ZACHARY *Taylor*

Zachary *Taylor*

OUR TWELFTH PRESIDENT

By Carol Brunelli

SPIRIT
of America™

The Child's World®, Inc.
Chanhassen, Minnesota

7

ZACHARY *Taylor*

Published in the United States of America by The Child's World®, Inc.
PO Box 326 • Chanhassen, MN 55317-0326 • 800-599-READ • www.childsworld.com

Acknowledgments

The Creative Spark: Mary Francis-DeMarois, Project Director; Elizabeth Sirimarco Budd, Series Editor; Robert Court, Design and Art Direction; Janine Graham, Page Layout; Jennifer Moyers, Production

The Child's World®, Inc.: Mary Berendes, Publishing Director; Red Line Editorial, Fact Research; Cindy Klingel, Curriculum Advisor; Robert Noyed, Historical Advisor

Photos

Cover: White House Collection, courtesy White House Historical Association; Art Resource: 10; The Library of Congress Collection: 6, 13, 14, 17, 19–23, 25–35; Independence National Historical Park: 8; Courtesy of the National Museum of the American Indian, Smithsonian Institution: 11 (P14027); Stock Montage: 7, 15

Registration

The Child's World®, Inc., Spirit of America™, and their associated logos are the sole property and registered trademarks of The Child's World®, Inc.

Library of Congress Cataloging-in-Publication Data

Brunelli, Carol.
  Zachary Taylor : our twelfth president / by Carol Brunelli.
     p. cm.
  Includes index.
  ISBN 1-56766-836-4 (alk. paper)
  1. Taylor, Zachary, 1784–1850—Juvenile literature. 2. Presidents—United States—Biography—Juvenile literature. [1. Taylor, Zachary, 1784–1850. 2. Presidents.]   I. Title.
  E422 .B89 2001
  973.6'3'092—dc21
                                                00-010571

15   25   34

Contents

Chapter ONE

Old Rough and Ready

Zachary Taylor was not a born politician, but his success as a soldier made him a hero. Many Americans believed he would make a good president.

ON NOVEMBER 24, 1784, ZACHARY TAYLOR was born in a cabin in his parents' native state of Virginia, but he would not stay there for long. His family was on its way to the new **frontier,** to unsettled lands in the state of Kentucky. The government gave Taylor's father a large piece of land for serving in the American Revolution. The Taylor family was traveling west across the Appalachian Mountains to start their new life. The Taylors and other **settlers** worked long days, carving their farms out of the thick forest. Taylor's earliest memories were of doing chores on his family's tobacco **plantation** with his eight brothers and sisters. Their plantation did well, as did their neighbors' plantations. But such success came with a price. The settlers were in Native American **territory.** If they wished to

keep the homes and farms for which they had worked so hard, they had to defend them against Native American attacks. From an early age, Zachary Taylor learned that America's new frontier was not only a place of great opportunity, but one of great danger as well.

Given his childhood experience with Native American warfare, it comes as no surprise that Taylor became a successful soldier later in life, nor is it surprising that he became a U.S. president. **Politics** and leadership ran in Taylor's family.

During the 19th century, Americans moved farther west onto Native American lands. When the Native Americans tried to turn these settlers back, violent conflicts arose.

Taylor's father, Richard, was a lieutenant colonel during the American Revolution. He served with General George Washington. Taylor's cousin, James Madison, was the fourth president of the United States. Another cousin, Robert E. Lee, later became the general in charge of the **Confederate** troops during the Civil War.

In 1808, James Madison, then the **secretary of state,** recommended Taylor for military service. The 23-year-old Taylor began a long, **distinguished** military service that would take him all the way to Washington, D.C. He first entered the army as a lieutenant in the **infantry.** Two years later, he married Margaret "Peggy" Mackall Smith on June 21, 1810. Their marriage lasted more than 40 years, and they had six children together. Taylor would spend nearly all of those years as a military officer.

As a soldier in the U.S. Army, Taylor's main responsibility was the protection of the frontier, which was expanding rapidly to the west. He defended the **Union** against foreign nations, such as Britain and Mexico. He also guarded against threats within the borders of the United States from Native American tribes.

In 1812, the United States declared war on Britain after many years of conflict. British troops and their Native American **allies** marched down from Canada and captured one American fort after another. On September 4, 450 Native Americans, led by a Shawnee chief named Tecumseh, surrounded Fort Harrison on the Wabash River in Indiana and lit one of the buildings on fire. Taylor quickly ordered that the burning roof be torn off to save the rest of the buildings. Taylor and his men put the fire out and then fought off Tecumseh's men. Indiana's governor praised Captain Taylor's "brave defense" of Fort Harrison, and the U.S. Army rewarded him with a **promotion** to the rank of major.

Taylor spent the next few years in retirement from the army. Soon, the nation would call on this soldier once again to keep peace in America's growing frontier. He spent much of the next 20 years training soldiers to defend forts along the Mississippi River in the present-day states of Iowa, Wisconsin, Minnesota, and Louisiana.

Tecumseh was a Shawnee chief known for being a fierce warrior. His name meant "Cougar Crouching for His Prey." During the War of 1812, he arrived at a battle just in time to see Native Americans brutally killing American prisoners. Tecumseh scolded the Native Americans and stopped the violence. He then turned to a British commander and called him a coward for allowing the murders to occur. This event made both Native American warriors and white soldiers respect the great leader.

In 1832, the army assigned Taylor (now a colonel) to lead U.S. soldiers once again. He took command of troops that were fighting a Native American war in the northwest corner of Illinois. More and more settlers in the region were moving onto Native American land. They were forcing the Sauk and the Fox tribes across the Mississippi River into Iowa.

10

Chief Black Hawk of the Sauk tribe was a brave Native American chief. During the War of 1812, the Sauks at first did not know if they were fighting with the British or with the Americans. In the past, members of the tribe had traded goods with both sides. But most of the Sauks favored siding with the British, who had promised to help protect the tribe's land.

Led by Chief Black Hawk of the Sauk tribe, the Native Americans fought to get back their land. Taylor's men did not want to follow the Native Americans onto unsettled lands, but he pushed them across Illinois and into the Wisconsin wilderness. The land was home to the Sauk and Fox. To Taylor's men, it was a wild, savage place. He later described how his

▶ During his many battles, Taylor often wore baggy cotton pants, a long coat, and a wide-brimmed straw hat instead of a uniform. His appearance and tough character earned him the nickname "Old Rough and Ready."

▶ Taylor's wife, Peggy, never sat for a portrait.

▶ Taylor didn't smoke or drink, but he enjoyed chewing tobacco.

men suffered, wading through "swamps and marshes" and passed over hills that would be considered "mountains in Europe." The soldiers' efforts paid off. A final battle, the Battle of Bad Axe, led to the surrender of the Sauk chief and his men. Colonel Taylor had put a stop to the war against Black Hawk and Sauk tribes.

In the state of Florida, the Seminole tribes had also tried to resist white settlement on their land. This led to the Second Seminole War, which lasted from 1835 to 1842. It was during this war that Taylor was given the nickname of "Rough and Ready." He showed himself to be unbeatable as he chased the Seminole through knee-deep mud and mosquito-infested swamps. The victory of Taylor's troops at the Battle of Okeechobee in 1837 earned him a promotion to general. He took command of all U.S. troops in Florida. Taylor gained great fame in this war for his rough-and-ready fighting. He still was not well known to most Americans, though. The next war Taylor fought—the Mexican War—would change that. He didn't know it at the time, but Taylor was on his way to the presidency.

THE ARMY OFTEN USED violence to force Native Americans from land that the U.S. government wanted to claim. This drawing shows Zachary Taylor during the Seminole War. Taylor and his troops sent bloodhounds to track the Native Americans. Taylor assured the government that the dogs would be used only to locate the Native Americans. Instead, the soldiers allowed the animals to viciously attack them.

Although American settlers wanted more land, not everybody approved of the government's way of getting it. In this drawing, which criticizes the brutal hunt, Taylor says the following to one of his soldiers:

> *Captain, We've got them at last, the dogs are at them … show no mercy—exterminate them … this day will close the Florida war, and write its history in the blood of the Seminole—but remember … I have written to our government to say that the dogs are intended to ferret out the Indians (not to worry them) … for the sake of consistency and the appearance of humanity, you will pretend not to notice the devastation they commit.*

Still, Taylor was known to be a fair man. He always honored **treaties** made with the Native Americans and prevented white settlers from spreading onto Native American lands. In fact, when Taylor's troops captured runaway slaves who were fighting with the Seminole, Taylor angered southerners by refusing to return them to their owners.

13

Chapter TWO

A National Hero

Just days after James Polk (above) became president in 1845, problems with Mexico grew serious. He sent General Zachary Taylor and U.S troops to the area.

FROM 1840 TO 1845, GENERAL ZACHARY Taylor retired from the frontier wars once again. He spent most of his time running his farms. Then President James K. Polk called his most trusted general back into service. A war was brewing between Mexico and the United States. General Taylor was to report to Texas immediately.

The problem first started in 1836 when Texas fought a war of independence with Mexico and won. After the war, Texas claimed that its southern border was the Rio Grande River. Mexico said the border was the Nueces River. Even before Texas was admitted to the Union on December 29, 1845, the United States and Mexico clashed in the disputed region.

Mexican soldiers with lances prepare to charge. Even though the Mexican force was much larger than that of the United States, American troops did well in battle from the very beginning of the Mexican War.

Taylor left his quiet life on the plantation and headed for Corpus Christi, Texas. From there, he marched his troops all the way to the banks of the Rio Grande. Taylor's troops arrived on March 28, 1846. They found a large Mexican army waiting for them just across the river. The armies waited and watched one another for weeks, adding more

▶ During Taylor's
time, sending mail
without stamps was
common because
it forced the recipient
to pay for postage.
Taylor told the post
office that he would
not accept letters with
postage due. He had
been receiving too
many of these from
admirers around the
country. Then the
Whigs sent him notice
without postage that
he had been chosen as
their **candidate** for
president. As a result,
Taylor didn't know
about his **nomination**
for several weeks, until
the Whigs sent him
another letter—this
time with postage.

troops to their armies. Then on April 24, 1846, hundreds of Mexican soldiers crossed the river. They surrounded a group of American soldiers. All the Americans were killed or captured. When word of this reached General Taylor, he quickly informed President Polk that the war with Mexico had begun. The U.S. officially declared war on May 13.

In battle after battle with Mexico, the American troops were outnumbered. Still, under the leadership of General Taylor, they never gave up or gave in. They won two big victories north of the Rio Grande in Texas and another in northern Mexico. Finally, Taylor marched his troops to a mountain pass near a ranch called Buena Vista. General Antonio López de Santa Anna and 15,000 Mexican soldiers headed his way. Taylor had just 4,600 men. He could have surrendered. After all, the odds were against a victory. But he refused to give up.

By all reports, it was his bravery that kept the troops in place under heavy fire and terrible odds. One officer raced up to the general and begged him to **retreat.** Taylor told him, "No, we will decide the battle here! I will, never,

16

alive, leave my wounded behind!" He moved fearlessly from one position to another on his horse, Old Whitey. He demanded bravery from his men.

The appearance of the general on the front line gave his soldiers courage. Two shots struck Taylor, one through his coat sleeve, the other through his coat. He barely noticed. He just continued to shout orders and watch the fighting. After two days of struggle, Santa Anna surrendered. Taylor had another unexpected victory.

Taylor led the Battle of Buena Vista on his trusted horse, Old Whitey. This event helped end the Mexican War. Although greatly outnumbered, the American forces would not give up.

In the United States, Americans were celebrating Taylor's victory at Buena Vista. He was a national hero. Some people believed the courageous man should run the country. Posters of "Rough and Ready" could be seen everywhere. Newspapers published stories about his military career and strong character. "Rough and Ready" clubs organized parades and **rallies** in support of a Taylor presidency. His popularity did not go unnoticed. It attracted the attention of the three major **political parties** of the day. Finally, Taylor decided to run with the Whig Party.

Presidential elections were just around the corner. Taylor had an excellent chance of winning. He was not only famous, he also was a man that Americans could admire. Old Rough and Ready was a national hero, but he looked like a normal, hardworking American farmer.

The Whig Party knew that Taylor would probably win on his popularity alone. They also knew his military record would win him votes with northerners, while the fact that he was a slave owner assured him southern votes. Taylor also didn't discuss his opinions about **controversial** topics—especially whether to

18

Americans loved General Taylor after his success in the Mexican War. His name and image showed up on advertisements and posters. This tobacco label features Rough and Ready on a battlefield during the Mexican War.

allow slavery in new states and territories. This kept him from making political enemies.

The Whig Party chose Millard Fillmore to run as the vice presidential candidate. Taylor's opponents were Lewis Cass of the Democratic Party and Martin Van Buren of the Free Soil Party. The main issue of the **campaign** was the Wilmot Proviso, which was a **bill** to **ban** slavery from any territory won in the Mexican War. Cass was against the Proviso, and Van Buren was for it. Taylor would not say where

19

Because Taylor was a southern slave owner, the Whig Party needed a vice presidential candidate who would please anti-slavery Whigs in the North. They chose New Yorker Millard Fillmore.

he stood on the issue. In the end, Taylor defeated Cass and Van Buren.

Zachary Taylor was sworn in on March 5, 1849, as the 12th president of the United States. At the time, no one really knew what he thought about the slavery issue. After all, he tried not to discuss difficult topics during his campaign. But Americans would find out what he thought soon enough. This time, he would state his opinion for all to hear.

20

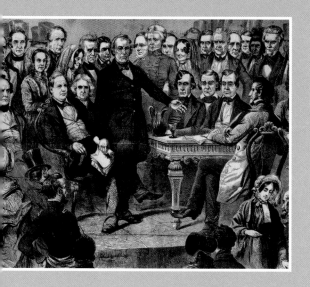

DURING THE PRESIDENTIAL CAMPAIGN OF 1848, FUTURE PRESIDENT Abraham Lincoln took part in the nomination and election of General Zachary Taylor. Lincoln made speeches in Maryland and Massachusetts, as well as in his home state of Illinois. He encouraged young men to become active in American politics by forming "Rough and Ready" clubs, groups that held meetings and made speeches in favor of a Zachary Taylor presidency. During the campaign, Lincoln wrote:

> Now as to the young men, you must not wait to be brought forward
> by the older men. For instance, do you suppose that I should ever
> have got into notice if I had waited to be hunted up and pushed
> forward by older men? You young men get together and form a
> "Rough and Ready" club, and have regular meetings and speeches.…
> Let every one play the part he can play best—some speak, some sing,
> and all "holler." Your meetings will be of evenings; the older men,
> and the women, will go to hear you; so that it will not only
> contribute to the election of "Old Zach," but will be an interesting
> pastime, and improving to the intellectual faculties of all engaged.

Lincoln's support and that of other important Americans of the day helped Taylor and Fillmore win the election. The image above shows the **inauguration** of Taylor on March 5, 1849.

21

Chapter THREE

Toward Ending Slavery

Zachary Taylor had little experience in politics. He had never held a political office before he became president. In fact, he had never even voted in an election. He once said he would be as happy "in a cabin as in the White House."

THE 1848 TREATY OF GUADALUPE HIDALGO ended the Mexican War. It also added new territories to the Union. These territories would eventually become states, but would they be free or slave states? That was the question the American people and Congress had to answer. The Missouri **Compromise** set the north-south border that divided the country into slave and free states. Not surprisingly, the South wanted this border to stretch all the way to the Pacific. The North wanted slavery banned in all new territories. There were fiery **debates** about this issue that would threaten the Union. But who was better prepared to defend the Union than the national hero, President Zachary Taylor?

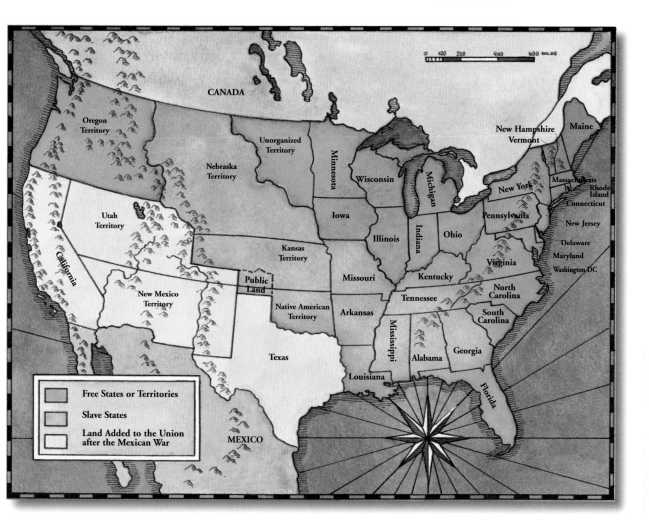

Taylor did not want to end slavery, but he **opposed** its spread to new territories. His position on slavery angered southerners. He was a southerner, had two plantations, and owned more than 100 slaves. How could he oppose slavery? How could he support the North?

Taylor did not support the North. He respected slaveholder's rights in the states where slavery was legal. But the spread of

After the Mexican War, the United States gained about 1.2 million square miles of new territory—all the land shaded yellow in the map above. But this forced the nation to face a serious problem: Would new states and territories allow slavery?

23

slavery was a very controversial subject. He thought it might tear apart the country, so he did not support it. To him, it was more important to **preserve** the Union than to extend slavery. He made his point clear when he said, "We must … preserve the Union at all hazards. Upon its preservation must depend our own happiness and that of countless generations to come. Whatever dangers may threaten it, I stand by it."

When the territories of California and New Mexico were settled, President Zachary Taylor encouraged them to quickly write their state **constitutions.** Then he said they should apply to become states. He hoped to avoid a debate over slavery by doing this, but he did not succeed. Southerners were angry because they knew those territories opposed slavery. Members of Congress were angry because they thought the president was trying to take away their right to make laws. During this time at the Capitol, there were heated debates over the slavery issue. Some congressmen even carried weapons, while others were involved in fistfights.

In the meantime, Senators John C. Calhoun of South Carolina, Daniel Webster

The Capitol, where Congress hotly debated the slavery issue, looked very different during President Taylor's time in office. In the 1860s, the much grander, taller dome of today replaced the wooden one shown here.

of Massachusetts, and Henry Clay of Kentucky were discussing ideas that would keep the North and South at peace. In 1850, Henry Clay introduced to Congress a set of **proposals.** These later became known as the Compromise of 1850. The proposals gave both the North and the South part of what they wanted. For example, California could join the Union as a free state to please the North. The Fugitive Slave Act was included to please the South. This act said the government had to make sure all runaway slaves were returned to their owners. Before this act, runaway slaves were free if they reached the North.

▶ On January 24th, 1848, just after Taylor's election, a man named James Marshall made a great discovery in the California territory. He found gold! Word of the discovery spread across the country. By 1849, thousands of gold seekers from the East moved into California, quickly settling the new territory. Because the year was 1849, these gold seekers were nicknamed the "forty-niners."

Taylor felt the compromise would allow the spread of slavery. He did not support any part of it that would favor the South. He wanted each proposal to be voted on separately. He hoped that some parts of it would pass and others would not. The proposals were debated in Congress, and some changes were made. The debate lasted until the final days of Taylor's presidency.

Senator Henry Clay, standing at center, introduced a compromise to Congress in 1850. He hoped to solve the slavery issue that was tearing the nation in two. He suggested giving both sides part of what they wanted. Taylor did not like the compromise. He refused to sign it into law.

THE WAR WITH Mexico greatly increased the territory of the United States and made some Americans hungry for more land. Spain controlled Cuba at the time. Some Cubans in the United States and southerners who wanted to expand slavery started a small movement to take over the island. Slavery was still legal in Cuba. The goal of the movement was to invade Cuba and make it part of the United States. Narciso Lopez, a former Cuban governor, led the movement. President Taylor heard about the group's plans. He warned them that if they moved ahead, they would have no protection from the United States and would be punished.

The group ignored the president's threat. Lopez set sail for Cuba from Mexico. Before reaching Cuba, 52 of his men were captured by the Spanish. Lopez and his remaining men finally arrived in Cardenas, Cuba (shown in the drawing above). There they found themselves heavily outnumbered by the Spanish troops. They turned around immediately, but the Spanish followed them. In the end, 70 Americans were killed.

True to his word, Taylor ordered the arrest of Lopez and his men. Taylor decided to help the 52 men who had been captured, however. They had not committed a crime, even though they had planned to do so. In exchange for their release, he promised the Spanish that the United States would help them keep control of Cuba. The men were freed, and Taylor avoided problems with Spain.

Chapter FOUR

Final Days of a Presidency

Zachary Taylor was the last candidate from the Whig Party to be elected president.

THE BIGGEST CRISIS OF ZACHARY TAYLOR'S presidency was whether to allow slavery to spread into new territories. This was not **resolved** during his brief 500 days as the president. But Taylor did have his accomplishments. The territory of the United States had greatly increased. The Department of the Interior was created during his presidency to manage the country's public lands. It also took charge of natural **resources** and Native American affairs. Perhaps the most important achievement during Taylor's presidency was an international one. Taylor and his assistants made sure that the United States would be able to use any Central American canals built in the future.

For some time, the United States had been planning the construction of a canal

Interesting Facts

▶ Taylor was the second president to die from illness while in office. William Henry Harrison, the ninth president, died of pneumonia just one month after his inauguration.

across Central America. Without a canal, ships had to sail around the southern tip of South America to travel from the Atlantic Ocean to the Pacific. In 1849, it appeared that Britain would take control of Central America. If this happened, any canal built there also would be under British control.

The British could refuse U.S. ships access to the canal or charge high fees for its use.

In 1850, the Clayton-Bulwer Treaty between the two nations guaranteed that any future canal constructed across Central America would be neutral. This meant that all nations would have fair and equal use of the canal. Eventually, the United States built a canal in Panama, which opened in 1914. Taylor's work on the treaty secured this important transportation route for future generations.

Zachary Taylor did not live to see the construction of a canal, nor did he resolve the debate over slavery. But he did hold together a nation that was growing and changing rapidly. If Taylor had been asked what his most important accomplishment was, he might have said it was

The Panama Canal (right) was not completed until 1914—more than 60 years after President Taylor's death. But it was a treaty during his term that ensured the United States could use it.

the preservation of the Union. He once said, "For more than half a century, during which kingdoms and empires have fallen, this Union has stood unshaken. The patriots who formed it have long since descended to the grave; yet still it remains, the proudest monument to their memory."

The Union stood unshaken in Taylor's time. Unfortunately, it would be torn apart 11 years later when the Civil War, the war between the North and South, began. Taylor did not live long enough to fight this war. On a hot and humid Independence Day, Taylor attended holiday ceremonies at the Washington Monument. He returned to the White House hot and exhausted. Trying to regain his strength, he ate a bowl of cherries and drank some iced

Zachary Taylor's plantation home in Kentucky is shown above. Taylor would never return to his home in the South. He died just 16 months after his inauguration.

milk. That evening, he had terrible stomach cramps. For the next five days, he became weaker from vomiting and diarrhea. Finally, on July 9, 1850, President Taylor died at 10:30 in the evening. The cause of his death was believed to be **inflammation** of the stomach and intestines. His doctors believed that either the milk or the cherries contained deadly bacteria. The following day, Vice

President Millard Fillmore took office as the 13th president of the United States.

Thousands of Americans lined the route of the funeral **procession.** Zachary Taylor's trusted horse, Old Whitey, followed behind the carriage that held the president's body.

Soon after his death, Congress passed the Compromise of 1850 with President Fillmore's support. But the debate over slavery was far

After President Taylor died, Millard Fillmore supported Clay's Compromise. The Senate passed it, briefly calming the nation. Journalist Walt Whitman called it "the last great effort" to save the nation, but it was not enough. The Civil War began 11 years later because the North and South could not resolve their differences.

Zachary Taylor had proven himself a strong and courageous man during his time in the U.S. Army. He faced many dangerous battles. Yet when a serious stomach illness overtook him, Taylor could not fight it. "In two days I shall be dead," he said.

Interesting Facts

▸ Taylor was president of the United States for less than 500 days.

▸ Taylor was a distant cousin of the 32nd president of the United States, Franklin D. Roosevelt, who was born 32 years after Taylor's death.

from over, as the Civil War would prove. Sadly, Taylor's only son, Richard, served as a general in the Confederate Army, the army that opposed the Union his father had fought so hard to protect.

34

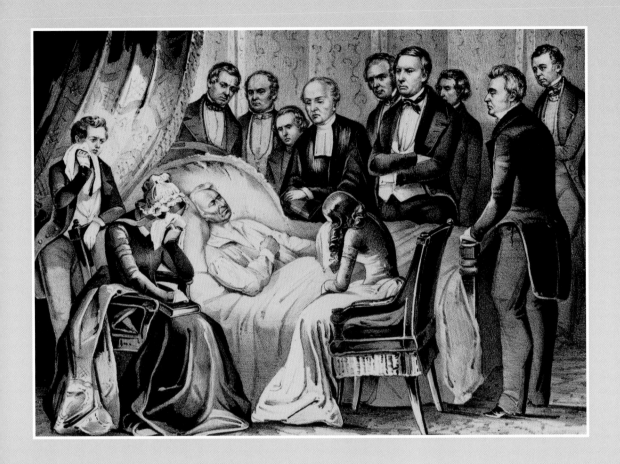

FOR YEARS, SOME HISTORIANS SUSPECTED THAT ZACHARY TAYLOR'S DEATH was not an accident. They believed he might have been murdered with arsenic, a deadly poison. In 1991, Taylor's **descendants** decided to find out the true cause of his death. Modern science can determine long after death if a person took poison. To test for the presence of arsenic, Taylor's remains were removed from the Zachary Taylor Memorial Cemetery in Louisville, Kentucky.

Samples of hair and fingernails were taken and tested in a laboratory. Scientists concluded that Taylor had indeed died of a severe stomach illness. This finding proved that Taylor's rivals were not guilty of murder.

35

1784 Taylor is born in Orange County, Virginia, near the town of Barboursville on November 24.

1785 The Taylor family settles in Beargrass Creek, near Louisville, Kentucky.

1790s Taylor is tutored at home in reading, writing, and arithmetic. He works on his family's tobacco plantation. In his spare time, he enjoys hunting, fishing, and riding horseback through the woods.

1808 On May 3, Taylor enters the U.S. Army as a first lieutenant in the infantry.

1810 On June 21, 25-year-old Taylor marries 21-year-old Margaret "Peggy" Mackall Smith. They will have five daughters and a son together.

1811 Taylor is promoted to the rank of captain and put in command of Fort Knox in the territory of Indiana.

1812 The United States declares war on Britain, starting the War of 1812. Taylor takes command of Fort Harrison in Indiana Territory. On September 4, he leads the defense and gains a victory against Shawnee Chief Tecumseh and his men. Taylor is promoted to the rank of major.

1816–1818 Taylor is sent to Fort Howard in present-day Green Bay, Wisconsin, to protect fur trappers in the area from attacks by Native Americans.

1819 Taylor is promoted to the rank of lieutenant colonel and is assigned to the southwest frontier of Louisiana.

1824 Taylor buys a 500-acre cotton plantation north of Baton Rouge, which includes 22 slaves.

1828 Taylor trains soldiers to defend various forts along the Mississippi River.

1832 Taylor is promoted to full colonel and takes command of part of an army in the wars against the Sauk tribe.

1835 The Second Seminole War begins. Taylor earns the nickname "Rough and Ready" during the war.

1838 Taylor fights his final battle against the Seminole at Lake Okeechobee and is promoted to rank of brigadier general.

1841 Taylor is put in charge of an area covering parts of the Louisiana, Arkansas, and Oklahoma territories. He oversees construction of forts and inspects border forts. In December, he buys a 2,100-acre plantation, Cypress Grove, in Jefferson County, Mississippi, and increases the number of slaves he owns to more than 100.

1845 President Polk sends Taylor to Texas to prepare for an invasion by Mexican forces. Problems have occurred between Americans and Mexicans in the area. On December 29, Texas becomes the 28th state to join the Union. Taylor moves his troops to the mouth of the Nueces River in Texas.

1846 Mexican forces attack U.S. forces in Texas on April 24. Taylor's men win the battles of Palo Alto and Resaca de la Palma. War is officially declared on May 13. Taylor is promoted to major general. Back in the nation's capital, a national debate over slavery begins after the Wilmot Proviso bill is introduced in Congress. The bill states that any land acquired from Mexico can never allow slavery.

1847 The Battle of Buena Vista begins on February 22. Taylor leads troops to victory and becomes a national hero.

1848 The Treaty of Guadalupe Hidalgo is signed on February 2, ending the war with Mexico. The Whig political party nominates Zachary Taylor as their presidential candidate. On November 7, Taylor is elected president of the United States. Before Taylor takes office, gold is discovered in California.

1849 Taylor resigns from the U.S. Army in January. On March 5, he is sworn in as the 12th president of the United States. The Department of the Interior is established. The California gold rush begins. Thousands of easterners known as the "forty-niners" go west to seek gold.

1850 Debates over the extension of slavery begin in Congress. Henry Clay introduces proposals known as "Clay's Compromise" to Congress. In April, the United States and Britain agree on the Clayton-Bulwer Treaty, which states that any canal built across Central America can be used by all nations. On July 4, Taylor falls ill with stomach cramps. After five days of suffering, he dies on July 9. Vice President Millard Fillmore is sworn in as the 13th president on July 10.

allies (AL-lize)
Allies are nations that have agreed to help each other by fighting together against a common enemy. During the War of 1812, the Shawnee tribe was a British ally, fighting against the United States.

ban (BAN)
To ban something means to make it illegal. People who did not support slavery wanted to ban it in the newest states to join the Union.

bill (BILL)
A bill is a proposed law presented to a group of lawmakers. Congress decides if a bill will become law.

campaign (kam-PAYN)
A campaign is the process of running for an election, including activities such as giving speeches or attending rallies. Abraham Lincoln supported Whig candidate Zachary Taylor during his 1848 campaign.

candidate (KAN-duh-det)
A candidate is a person running in an election. Several candidates run for president every four years.

compromise (KOM-pruh-myz)
A compromise is a way to settle a disagreement in which both sides give up part of what they want. The U.S. Senate created the Compromise of 1850 in an attempt to satisfy both the North and the South.

Confederate (kun-FED-ur-ut)
Confederate refers to the slave states (or the people who lived in those states) that left the Union in 1861. The people of the South were called Confederates.

constitutions (kon-stih-TOO-shunz)
Constitutions are the sets of basic principles that govern a state, country, or society. California's constitution outlawed slavery.

controversial (kon-truh-VUR-shul)
If something is controversial, people disagree and argue about it. A controversial topic in the election of 1848 was the expansion of slavery into the land acquired by the United States after the Mexican War.

Glossary TERMS

debates (deh-BAYTZ)
Debates are arguments about a certain subject. In 1850, there were heated debates in Congress about Henry Clay's compromise proposals.

descendants (dee-SEN-dentz)
Descendants are people born after someone else within the same family, such as children and grandchildren. Taylor's descendants believed he might have been poisoned.

distinguished (deh-STING-gwisht)
If someone is distinguished, he or she is well known for positive accomplishments or deeds. Zachary Taylor was a distinguished military leader in the United States Army.

frontier (frun-TEER)
A frontier is a region that is at the edge of or beyond settled land. During Zachary Taylor's lifetime, the American frontier was rapidly expanding westward.

inauguration (ih-naw-gyuh-RAY-shun)
An inauguration is the ceremony that takes place when a new president begins a term. Taylor died just 16 months after his inauguration.

infantry (IN-fun-tree)
An infantry is a group of soldiers trained to fight on foot. Zachary Taylor first entered the army in the infantry.

inflammation (in-fluh-MAY-shun)
Inflammation is when part of the body becomes diseased, usually marked by swelling and pain. Taylor died from inflammation of the stomach.

nomination (nom-ih-NAY-shun)
If someone receives a nomination, he or she is chosen by a political party to run for an office, such as the presidency.

oppose (uh-POHZ)
If people oppose something, they are against it. President Taylor opposed the spread of slavery into new territories.

plantation (plan-TAY-shun)
A plantation is a large farm or group of farms that grows crops such as tobacco, sugarcane, or cotton. Zachary Taylor was a southern plantation owner and a slaveholder.

**political parties
(puh-LIT-uh-kul PAR-teez)**
Political parties are groups of people who share similar ideas about how to run a government. Members of the Whig political party opposed the Democratic Party.

politics (PAWL-uh-tiks)
Politics refers to the actions and practices of the government. Taylor started his career in the military, not in politics.

preserve (pree-ZERV)
If people preserve something, they keep it from harm or change. Taylor believed it was more important to preserve the Union than to extend slavery.

procession (proh-SEH-shun)
A procession is a group of people or vehicles moving along in a line. More than 100 carriages traveled in President Taylor's funeral procession.

promotion (pruh-MOH-shun)
When people get a promotion, they advance in rank or importance. The U.S. Army rewarded Taylor with promotions to higher ranks.

proposals (pruh-POH-zulz)
Proposals are suggested plans or ideas. Senator Henry Clay's proposals, later known as the Compromise of 1850, were discussed for many months before Congress passed them.

rallies (RAL-eez)
Rallies are organized gatherings of people to show support for something or someone. In 1848, there were "Rough and Ready" political rallies for Whig presidential candidate Zachary Taylor.

resolve (ree-ZOLV)
If people resolve a problem, they find a successful solution to it. The slavery issue was not resolved during Taylor's presidency.

resources (REE-sor-sez)
Resources are things that can be used to benefit people, such as oil or water. The government often controls land with valuable natural resources.

retreat (ree-TREET)
If an army retreats, it moves back or withdraws to avoid danger or defeat. At the battle of Buena Vista, General Taylor refused to retreat, even though American forces were outnumbered.

secretary of state (SEK-ruh-tair-ee OF STAYT)
The secretary of state is a close advisor to the president of the United States on relations with other countries. As secretary of state in 1808, James Madison recommended Taylor for military service.

settlers (SET-lurz)
Settlers are people who set up a home in a new place. American settlers who moved to the new frontier built their own houses, farms, and villages.

territory (TAIR-ih-tor-ee)
A territory is a land or region, especially land that belongs to a government. As Americans settled the new frontier, they found that many different Native American tribes already inhabited the territory.

treaties (TREE-teez)
Treaties are formal agreements between nations. The United States and Britain agreed on the Clayton-Bulwer treaty.

union (YOON-yen)
A union is the joining together of two or more people or groups of people, such as states. The Union is another name for the United States.

Our PRESIDENTS

President	Birthplace	Life Span	Presidency	Political Party	First Lady
George Washington	Virginia	1732–1799	1789–1797	None	Martha Dandridge Custis Washington
John Adams	Massachusetts	1735–1826	1797–1801	Federalist	Abigail Smith Adams
Thomas Jefferson	Virginia	1743–1826	1801–1809	Democratic-Republican	widower
James Madison	Virginia	1751–1836	1809–1817	Democratic Republican	Dolley Payne Todd Madison
James Monroe	Virginia	1758–1831	1817–1825	Democratic Republican	Elizabeth Kortright Monroe
John Quincy Adams	Massachusetts	1767–1848	1825–1829	Democratic-Republican	Louisa Johnson Adams
Andrew Jackson	South Carolina	1767–1845	1829–1837	Democrat	widower
Martin Van Buren	New York	1782–1862	1837–1841	Democrat	widower
William H. Harrison	Virginia	1773–1841	1841	Whig	Anna Symmes Harrison
John Tyler	Virginia	1790–1862	1841–1845	Whig	Letitia Christian Tyler / Julia Gardiner Tyler
James K. Polk	North Carolina	1795–1849	1845–1849	Democrat	Sarah Childress Polk

Our PRESIDENTS

President	Birthplace	Life Span	Presidency	Political Party	First Lady
Zachary Taylor	Virginia	1784–1850	1849–1850	Whig	Margaret Mackall Smith Taylor
Millard Fillmore	New York	1800–1874	1850–1853	Whig	Abigail Powers Fillmore
Franklin Pierce	New Hampshire	1804–1869	1853–1857	Democrat	Jane Means Appleton Pierce
James Buchanan	Pennsylvania	1791–1868	1857–1861	Democrat	never married
Abraham Lincoln	Kentucky	1809–1865	1861–1865	Republican	Mary Todd Lincoln
Andrew Johnson	North Carolina	1808–1875	1865–1869	Democrat	Eliza McCardle Johnson
Ulysses S. Grant	Ohio	1822–1885	1869–1877	Republican	Julia Dent Grant
Rutherford B. Hayes	Ohio	1822–1893	1877–1881	Republican	Lucy Webb Hayes
James A. Garfield	Ohio	1831–1881	1881	Republican	Lucretia Rudolph Garfield
Chester A. Arthur	Vermont	1829–1886	1881–1885	Republican	widower
Grover Cleveland	New Jersey	1837–1908	1885–1889	Democrat	Frances Folsom Cleveland

President	Birthplace	Life Span	Presidency	Political Party	First Lady
Benjamin Harrison	Ohio	1833–1901	1889–1893	Republican	Caroline Scott Harrison
Grover Cleveland	New Jersey	1837–1908	1893–1897	Democrat	Frances Folsom Cleveland
William McKinley	Ohio	1843–1901	1897–1901	Republican	Ida Saxton McKinley
Theodore Roosevelt	New York	1858–1919	1901–1909	Republican	Edith Kermit Carow Roosevelt
William H. Taft	Ohio	1857–1930	1909–1913	Republican	Helen Herron Taft
Woodrow Wilson	Virginia	1856–1924	1913–1921	Democrat	Ellen L. Axson Wilson / Edith Bolling Galt Wilson
Warren G. Harding	Ohio	1865–1923	1921–1923	Republican	Florence Kling De Wolfe Harding
Calvin Coolidge	Vermont	1872–1933	1923–1929	Republican	Grace Goodhue Coolidge
Herbert C. Hoover	Iowa	1874–1964	1929–1933	Republican	Lou Henry Hoover
Franklin D. Roosevelt	New York	1882–1945	1933–1945	Democrat	Anna Eleanor Roosevelt Roosevelt
Harry S. Truman	Missouri	1884–1972	1945–1953	Democrat	Elizabeth Wallace Truman

Our PRESIDENTS

President	Birthplace	Life Span	Presidency	Political Party	First Lady
Dwight D. Eisenhower	Texas	1890–1969	1953–1961	Republican	Mary "Mamie" Doud Eisenhower
John F. Kennedy	Massachusetts	1917–1963	1961–1963	Democrat	Jacqueline Bouvier Kennedy
Lyndon B. Johnson	Texas	1908–1973	1963–1969	Democrat	Claudia Alta Taylor Johnson
Richard M. Nixon	California	1913–1994	1969–1974	Republican	Thelma Catherine Ryan Nixon
Gerald Ford	Nebraska	1913–	1974–1977	Republican	Elizabeth "Betty" Bloomer Warren Ford
James Carter	Georgia	1924–	1977–1981	Democrat	Rosalynn Smith Carter
Ronald Reagan	Illinois	1911–	1981–1989	Republican	Nancy Davis Reagan
George Bush	Massachusetts	1924–	1989–1993	Republican	Barbara Pierce Bush
William Clinton	Arkansas	1946–	1993–2001	Democrat	Hillary Rodham Clinton
George W. Bush	Connecticut	1946–	2001–	Republican	Laura Welch Bush

Presidential FACTS

Qualifications

To run for president, a candidate must
- be at least 35 years old
- be a citizen who was born in the United States
- have lived in the United States for 14 years

Term of Office

A president's term of office is four years. No president can stay in office for more than two terms.

Election Date

The presidential election takes place every four years on the first Tuesday of November.

Inauguration Date

Presidents are inaugurated on January 20.

Oath of Office

I do solemnly swear I will faithfully execute the office of the President of the United States and will to the best of my ability preserve, protect, and defend the Constitution of the United States.

Write a Letter to the President

One of the best things about being a U.S. citizen is that Americans get to participate in their government. They can speak out if they feel government leaders aren't doing their jobs. They can also praise leaders who are going the extra mile. Do you have something you'd like the president to do? Should the president worry more about the environment and encourage people to recycle? Should the government spend more money on our schools? You can write a letter to the president to say how you feel!

1600 Pennsylvania Avenue
Washington, D.C. 20500

You can even send an e-mail to: president@whitehouse.gov

For Further INFORMATION

Internet Sites

Read Taylor's inaugural address:
http://www.bartleby.com/124/pres28.html

Read Taylor's letter offering himself as a presidential candidate:
http://www.americanpresidents.org/letters/12.asp

Find more links to sites about Zachary Taylor:
http://sss.encarta.msn.com/index/conciseindex/12/012BE000.htm

Find out more about the Mexican War:
http://www.geocities.com/Athens/Academy/9110/mexicanwar.htm

Find out more about frontier life in the 19th century:
http://www.system.missouri.edu/whmc/pioneer.htm

Learn more about all the presidents:
http://www.whitehouse.gov/WH/glimpse/presidents/html/presidents/html
http://www.thepresidency.org/presinfo.htm
http://www.americanpresidents.org

Books

Nancy Bonvillain. *Black Hawk, Sac Rebel* (North American Indians of Achievement). Broomall, PA: Chelsea House, 1993.

Cwiklik, Robert, and W. David Baird. *Tecumseh: Shawnee Rebel* (North American Indians of Achievement). Broomall, PA: Chelsea House, 1993.

DeGregorio, William A. *The Complete Book of U.S. Presidents.* New York: Random House, 1997.

Jacobs, William Jay. *War with Mexico* (Spotlight on American History). Brookfield, CT: Millbrook Press, 1993.

Kent, Zachary. *Zachary Taylor* (Encyclopedia of Presidents). Danbury, CT: Childrens Press, 1988.

Paulson, Timothy, and Darlene Clark Hine. *Days of Sorrow, Years of Glory 1831–1850: From Nat Turner Revolt to the Fugitive Slave Law* (Milestones in Black American History). Broomall, PA: Chelsea House Publishers, 1994.

Index